COLLECTIONS

A Harcourt Reading Program

Blue Skies

Harcourt

Orlando   Boston   Dallas   Chicago   San Diego

Visit *The Learning Site!*

www.harcourtschool.com

CONTENTS

THE LOUD RIDE

by Susan McCloskey
illustrated by Lisa Campbell Ernst

"TAP!" said Jan. "TAP, TAP!"

"What is that?" said Dad.

"I am reading a story," said Jan.

"I like this story," she said. "It is loud."

"It IS loud," said Dad. "I never knew books could be so loud."

"RAP!" said Sam. "RAP, RAP!"

"What is that?" said Dad.

"I am reading a story," said Sam.

"I like this story," he said. "It is noisy."

"It IS noisy," said Dad. "I never knew books could be so noisy."

"BAM!" said Pam. "BAM, BAM!"

"What is that?" said Dad.

"I am reading a story," said Pam.

"I like this story," she said. "It is loud."

"It IS loud," said Dad. "I never knew books could be so loud."

"Look!" said Dad.
"Do you see that? The van cannot go. I wonder what we can do now."

"Do not get angry, Dad," said Jan.

"No, do not get mad," said Sam and Pam.

"We have an idea."

"How do you like the idea, Dad?" they said.
Dad grinned.
"It is not bad," he said.
"It is not a bad idea at all!"

"TAP!" said Jan.

"RAP!" said Sam.

"BAM!" said Pam.

"TAP, TAP, RAP, RAP, BAM, BAM!" they all said.

"There they go!" said Dad. "I am not surprised. They never knew books could be so noisy!"

Think About It

1. What do Jan, Sam, and Pam do so that the van can go?

2. Before the ride in the van, what did Dad think about books?

3. What could Dad do to make the next ride less noisy? Write your idea.

A Walk in the Woods

by Barbara Diaz
illustrated by David McPhail

Kim and Tip loved fall. They loved to
go for walks in the woods.

Kim loved walking in the fall leaves.
Tip loved sniffing the fall leaves.

Kim loved the apple trees south of the woods. She picked some apples.

Tip loved chipmunks. He loved looking for chipmunks.

"Look over there, Tip!" said Kim.

"I see a chipmunk! Can you find his tree?"

"Look at the chipmunk zip up that big tree!" said Kim. "We will sit for a bit."

Kim and Tip did not make a noise.

Then Kim said, "When will you come down, chipmunk?" They could see the chipmunk, but it did not come down.

"We have to go, Tip," said Kim.

"We have to walk back. I loved picking apples. You loved sniffing leaves. And you and I loved seeing a chipmunk!"

Think About It

1. Why do Kim and Tip take a walk in the woods? What do they do?
2. Why doesn't the chipmunk come down from the tree?
3. What could Kim and Tip do in the woods in winter? Write your idea.

Setting

The time and place in which a story happens is the **setting.** The pictures and words in a story help you know the setting.

The setting of "A Walk in the Woods" is the woods in the fall. This web shows some of the things that help you know the setting.

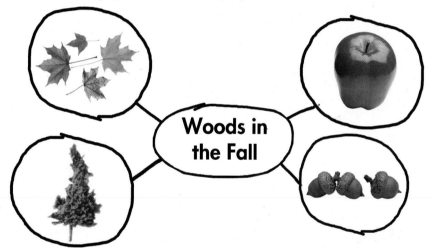

Woods in the Fall

You could read a story in which a class looks outside at the snow. Think about the time and place. What would be the setting of that story?

You could write a story about what you do for fun in the summer. Draw a web to tell about the setting of your story.

One Fine Night

by Jean Groce

illustrated by Gregg Valley

Hal sat alone.

"Being at home all alone is sad," he said. "But there is no reason to be alone. I will call Rip."

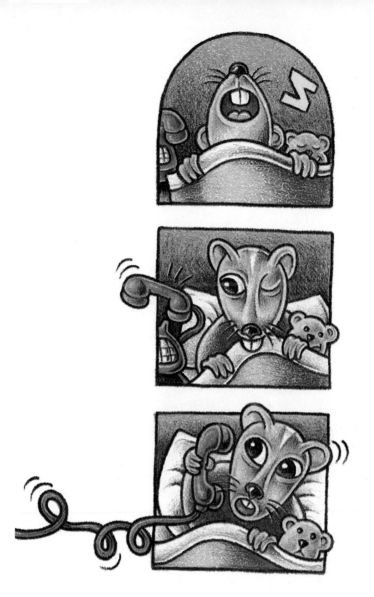

"I am sad to be all alone, Rip," said Hal.
"Come over!"

"Sorry," said Rip. "I'm napping. Call when I'm
not napping."

Hal sat alone. "There's no reason to be alone," he said. "I will call Mack."

"Come over, Mack, my friend!" he said. "I don't like to be alone."

"Sorry," said Mack. "I'm digging in the meadow. Call when I'm not digging."

Hal sat alone. "There's no reason to be alone," he said. "I will call Gil."

"I am glad I found you at home, Gil," he said. "Can you come over? I'm sad because I'm alone."

"Sorry," said Gil. "I have to swim in the river. I cannot come out."

"My nap is spoiled now," said Rip. "Hal is sad. I will call and cheer him up."

"I have had it with digging," said Mack. "I will find Hal. He does not like to be alone."

"I could zip down the river alone," said Gil, "but I'm going to call Hal. He is sad because he is alone."

Being alone is fine for some.
Being with friends is fine for all.
It is fine to have friends!

Think About It

1. Why do Rip, Mack, and Gil go to see their friend Hal?
2. Why doesn't Hal like to be alone?
3. Make a list of things Hal can do alone if his friends can't see him.

Just You and Me

by Bill E. Neder   illustrated by Jeremy Tugeau

I had no friends at school. The kids
clustered in groups. They ran and roared.
But I never played in the groups.

Mom said, "Make a friend at school."

Dad said, "Make a friend at school."

So I did make a friend—a snow
friend. My snow friend was Bob.

How did I make my snow friend Bob?
It was a big job!

I gathered snow into balls. Then I sat a
ball on a ball on a ball!

I got a pot for a hat. Then I got
a mop.

My snow friend Bob was my one
friend at school. We played a lot. I
could jog, and Bob watched. I could
hop, and Bob watched. I sat at my
desk, and Bob watched.

What a friend Bob was!

The kids gathered to see my snow
friend. Some wandered over to look.
Some raced over. They all loved Bob
a lot!

They said, "How did you make
that snow friend?"

One kid said, "Come and be in
my group!"

Then all the kids said, "No, play in my
group!"

I played and played in all the groups.

It is hot now. There is no snow. I sit at my desk and look out. Bob is not there. A snow friend cannot be there when it is hot.

I am not sad. I have friends at school now. When the snow comes back, we can all make snow friends!

Think About It

1. How does the boy in the story make a friend?

2. Why can't Bob be there when it is hot?

3. If Bob could talk, what would he say to the boy? What would he say to the rest of the kids? Write Bob's speech.

Characters' Feelings and Actions

Story characters have feelings, just as you do. When you read, think about what the characters do and say. This will help you know how the characters feel.

Look at these pictures from "Just You and Me." Pictures help you know about feelings, too. How does the boy feel at first? How does he feel at the end of the story?

Make up a story character. Draw a picture to show how the character feels. Then write a sentence to tell what the character does and says. Share your picture and sentence with a partner.

Turtle Makes a Wish

by Anne W. Phillips   illustrated by Lisa Guy

Turtle had a home in the river.
He could swim with Fish.
He could snap up an ant, like Frog.
But Turtle was small and dull.
"I am not tall," said Turtle. "I am not
handsome. I hardly like myself at all."

There was a zoo at the river. In the zoo, Turtle could see lots of animals. Turtle spotted a tall animal.

"I wish I could be tall," said Turtle. "I wish my wish could come true."

Turtle's wish did come true.
He got so tall!

Now Turtle could look sideways and up
and down. He could see animals all over
the zoo.

"How exciting!" said Turtle.
"But I am still not handsome."

Turtle spotted a handsome animal.
"I wish I could be handsome," said
Turtle. "I wish my wish could come true."
Turtle's wish did come true.
He got so handsome!
He was not dull now. He was sparkling!

"Who are you?" said the animals in the river.

"I'm Turtle," said Turtle.

"Turtle swims in the river," said Fish. "You cannot swim like Turtle."

"Turtle snaps up an ant when he is hungry," said Frog. "You cannot snap like Turtle."

Turtle was sad.

"I wish I could be myself," he said. "I wish my wish could come true."

Turtle's wish did come true.

He could swim.

He could snap up an ant when he was hungry.

He could play with his friends.

"Turtle, we are so glad to see you," said his friends.

"I am glad to be back to myself," said Turtle.

Think About It

1. Why don't the river friends like the tall, handsome Turtle?

2. What does Turtle find out when his wishes come true?

3. What if Fish wished to get out of the river and be on the land? What do you think Turtle would say to his friend? Write a letter from Turtle to Fish.

A Turnip's Tale

by Lois Bick

illustrated by Holly Cooper

A woman planted a turnip on a hill.

The turnip grew and grew.

It was enormous!

It got so big it tipped over.

Then down, down, down the hill it fell.

The turnip fell into a well.
What a mess!
"Oh, no! That turnip is in my well!"
the woman yelled. "I have to get it out!"

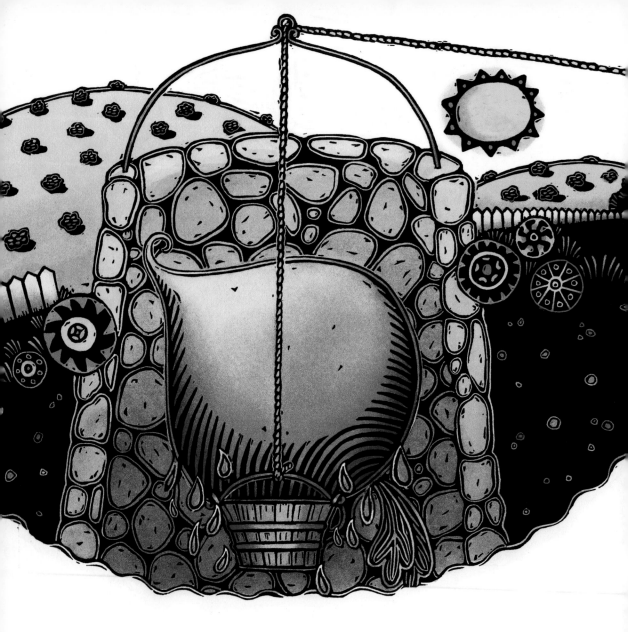

The woman pulled and pulled. Then she
pulled again.

But she could not get the turnip out of
the well.

She called for help.

"I will help," her granddaughter said.

The woman and her granddaughter pulled and pulled. Then they pulled again.

But they could not get the turnip out of the well.

The granddaughter called for help.

"We will help," some men said.

The woman and her granddaughter and the men pulled and pulled. Then they pulled again.

But they could not get the turnip out of the well.

The men called for help.

"I can help," said a mouse.

"You?" the woman asked. "You are a little pest. You are not strong."

"Well, I will do my best," the mouse said. "Look. Then do what I do."

The mouse bent over the well. Then all the rest helped.

Yes! They got the turnip out!
The woman was so glad!
The granddaughter clapped her hands.
The men sat down to rest.
The little mouse had a big grin.
He did his best, and he got that turnip out!

Think About It

1. How does the mouse get the turnip out of the well?

2. Why does the woman think that the mouse can't help?

3. What will the woman do the next time she plants a turnip? Draw your idea.

Sequence

Most stories tell about things in time order. You read about what happens first, next, and after that. At the end, you read about what happens last.

In "A Turnip's Tale," these things happen first.

A woman plants a turnip.

The turnip grows to be enormous.

The turnip falls down a hill into a well.

The woman tries to get the turnip out of the well.

What happens next in the story? What is the last thing that happens?

Think of something you would like to do. Plan to tell about the things that will happen in time order. Make a chart to show your plan.

TOOLS THAT HELP

by Beverly A. Dietz
photographs by Ken Kinzie

We found out what chores kids like to do.

54

Ted likes helping his mom. Ted said, "I like digging with my tools. I work alongside my mom. She tells me what to do. I wish for the plants to sprout."

55

Doing the dishes is Jim's chore.
Jim said, "This is a simple job. I
do not get paid, but I like
helping out at home. This tool
helps me do the job."

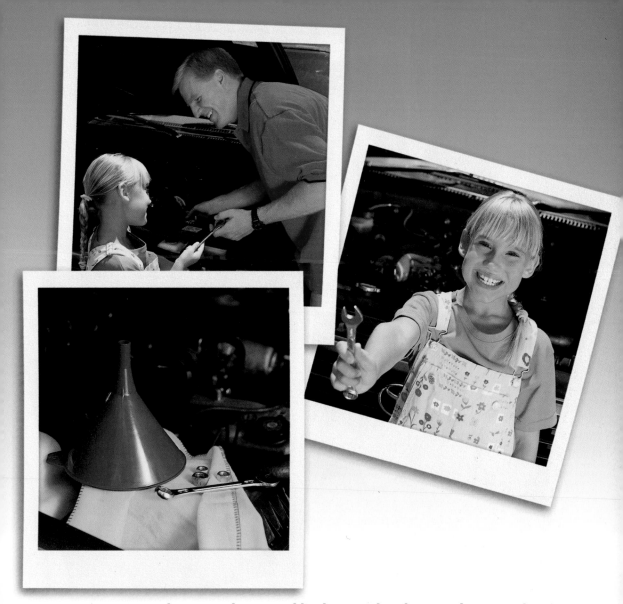

Tish works with her dad. Tish said, "My dad has to fix this engine. It's a job for an adult. Dad gets paid to do this work. I work alongside him. I get his tools for him. I am learning what to do."

Ben helped do this job. He said,
"I worked with an adult and some
kids. We all had tools like this."

Pat's chore is walking Shep. Pat
said, "This job is like playing. I
go out with Shep, and we walk
and walk. This tool helps!"

What chores do you do?
What tools help you do
the jobs you like?

Think About It

1. What are three chores the kids in the story do?

2. How is Pat's job like playing?

3. Draw a picture of a tool that helps you do a chore. Write about that chore.

The Promise

by Susan McCloskey

illustrated by Laura Freeman

Crump's Toy Shop was packed.

Lun was there with his mom.

"Mr. Crump, will this plane's engine start?" asked Lun.

"No, but this plane's will," said Mr. Crump. "Here are the directions."

So Lun and his mom bought that one.

Bud was in the toy shop with his dad.

"Mr. Crump, will this crane's engine start?" asked Bud.

"No, but this crane's engine will," said Mr. Crump. "Here are the directions."

So Bud and his dad bought that one.

Mr. Crump's cat, Muffin, was sitting
in the sun.

She was tugging one of the toys.

What was that buzz? What was that hum?

Muffin twitched. She looked up. It was a
bug! She liked bugs.

Muffin jumped up. What fun!

"That cat can run!" said Bud.

"Yes," said his dad, "but that bug can fly."

"That cat can jump," said Lun.

"Yes," said his mom, "but that bug can fly."

Mr. Crump said, "The bug can fly. Muffin can't, but do not worry. She'll get that bug. That's a promise!"

The bug landed on a plane. So did Muffin.
Smash! The plane was flat.
The bug landed on a shelf. So did Muffin.
Crash! The toys spilled all over.
Muffin looked for the bug. Was it in the
rug? She dug and dug.

At last Muffin grabbed the bug.

She dropped it into Mr. Crump's hand.

Mr. Crump hugged Muffin. Then he
let the bug go.

So long, bug!

Lun helped Mr. Crump pick up the toys.

"Muffin has a lot of fun hunting for bugs!"
Lun said.

Mr. Crump grinned. "Yes. Muffin likes to
hunt. She will not stop until she gets her bug.
That's a promise!"

Muffin sat in the sun. What was that buzz?
What was that hum? It was a bug!

What fun! Muffin liked bugs.

Think About It

1. What does Mr. Crump promise that Muffin will do?

2. Do you think Muffin catches every bug she chases? Why or why not?

3. What could happen to Muffin if she catches a bug that stings or bites? Draw your idea.

Too Many Cupcakes

by Deborah Eaton
illustrated by Jim Paillot

Knock, knock, knock!

Possum was at the kitchen door.

"Possum!" said Rabbit. "I am glad to see you. Come in and shut the door. We can make cupcakes!"

"Cupcakes?" said Possum. "I think cupcakes are grand!"

Rabbit was a whiz in the kitchen.

Possum was not.

Rabbit got the recipe for a buttery yellow cake.

Possum got the bowl.

Thud! Thump! Wham! Crash!

The bowl cracked into small bits. What a mess!

"Now what?" asked Possum.

"The bathtub!" said Rabbit.

"The bathtub?" asked Possum.

The bathtub was like a big bowl.
Rabbit mixed the thick batter.
Possum added this and that.
He mixed the batter with Rabbit.
Then Possum fell in! What a mess!

Possum had batter smeared all over him.

"Rabbit!" he said. "I took a bath in the batter!"

"Come on," said Rabbit. "We have to get the cupcakes into the oven. It's hot now."

Back to the kitchen they went.

Rabbit tipped the oven door just a bit.

The cupcakes got hot. So did the batter on Possum!

"Perfect!" said Rabbit.

Possum looked a bit sad.

"You are a whiz in the kitchen, Rabbit," he said. "But I am not. I just make a mess."

"That's OK, Possum," Rabbit said. "There are a lot of cupcakes, my friend. You will be a whiz at helping me finish them!"

Think About It

1. What did Rabbit do in the bathtub? Why?

2. At the end of the story, why was Possum sad?

3. Rabbit and Possum have decided to invite their friends to a cupcake party. Write an invitation telling when and where the party will be.

Synonyms and Antonyms

Synonyms are words that have almost the same meaning.

Antonyms are words that have opposite meanings.

Read these sentences:

I am glad to see you.

I am happy to see you.

The words *glad* and *happy* are synonyms. They almost have the same meaning.

Now read this sentence:

I am sad to see you.

The words *glad* and *sad* are antonyms. They have opposite meanings.

Draw a picture of a small animal. Write about the animal. Use the words *small* and *glad* in your sentences.

Then change your sentences. Use antonyms for *small* and *glad*. Draw a new picture to go with your new sentences.

A Lemonade Surprise

by Julia Miguel

illustrated by Ed Martinez

Barb was glum.

Her mom said, "What's wrong? Don't you like this home?"

"I do like it," said Barb. "I just miss my friends."

"You'll make friends in school," said Mom.

Barb spotted some kids in the next yard.

"Go on over," Mom said. "Ask if they'd like some lemonade."

"OK," said Barb. She grabbed some cups and the jug of lemonade. Then she went next door.

"Thanks for the lemonade!" said the kids.

"You're welcome," said Barb. "What's that?"

"That *was* a clubhouse," Mark announced. "It fell down."

"We can't rebuild it," added Kim. "The club has no money."

"I'm sorry," said Barb. "I wish I could help."

Karl sipped his lemonade. Then he grinned.

"We can make money with this and this," he said. "We can set up a stand and sell lemonade."

"Let's get started!" the club members yelled.

Karl and Kim set up a stand.

Barb was glad she could help. She and Mark mixed lemonade in her kitchen. Mom let them have cups.

"Come and get it!" Karl called. "Fresh lemonade!"

Adults and children arrived at the stand. The sales went on all day. At last the jugs were empty. Barb added up the money.

"We did it!" she said. "We can rebuild the clubhouse."

Barb went over to the clubhouse. On the door was a card. It said "JUST MEMBERS."

Now Barb was glum again. She was not a member of the club. She started to go home, but the kids stopped her.

"Don't go," they said. "You're a friend. *All* friends are members of *this* club."

Think About It

1. How does Barb make new friends?
2. How do you know Barb has just moved to a new neighborhood?
3. Make a list of steps for making lemonade. Use words and drawings.

Anna's Apple Dolls

by Meish Goldish

illustrated by Tom Casmer

Setting: *A frontier cabin in the west.*

| Dad | Mom | Garth | Mitch |

| Kip | Charles | Anna |

Anna: Mom?

Mom: What is it, Anna?

Anna: I did all my work. May I go outdoors now? May I play in the apple orchard?

Mom: Yes, you may, Anna. Take a basket and get some apples, too. Get a big batch for the family.

Anna: All right. I'll bring as many as I can.

(*Anna takes a basket and walks out.*)

Setting: *On the path to the orchard.*

Charles: Well, look who's here! It's little Anna!

Kip: Anna! Why are you outdoors? A wild animal may be nearby. It could catch you!

Mitch: Could you survive, Anna? Could you tame a wild animal?

Garth: All right, you three. Let Anna be. She is your sis, after all.

Anna: Yes, and I can work just as hard as you can!

Charles: Can you chop a tree?

Kip: Can you dig a ditch?

Mitch: Can you catch a fish?

Anna: No, but I can pick apples for our family. I'll pick a big batch of them! You just watch and see.

Garth: I'll go with you, Anna. We'll have fun picking apples.

(Anna and Garth walk away.)

Setting: *Outdoors at the orchard.*

Anna: These trees are so tall, Garth! Which apples will you pick? Watch what you are doing up there. Your feet may slip.

Garth: I'm OK, Anna. We can get lots of apples here!

(Garth hands an apple to Anna. She stops to look at it.)

Anna: Garth, do you know what? This apple looks a little bit like a doll. I think I could make it into a doll.

(Anna sets down her basket. She sits down.)

Anna: Come, little doll. I will put two seeds here so you can see. Next I will put seeds over your chin so you can grin! Now here are sticks for your arms and your legs and feet. I think Mom will stitch a dress for you. I will ask for a hat to match! You will be my apple doll. The family will like you!

Garth: Anna, let's go home. It's getting dark.

(Anna takes the doll and Garth takes her basket. They run home.)

Setting: *The family cabin.*

Anna: Mom! Dad! Look what I made!

(The family looks at Anna's doll.)

Dad: Why, Anna! That's so good!

Charles: I like it! You made an apple doll!

Kip: I like what you did with the seeds!

Mitch: I like her feet!

Garth: I bet there is no doll like it in all the West!

Mom: Anna, your friends will want dolls like this. You can help them make apple dolls, too.

Anna: Yes! We can all have apple dolls. That will be fun!

Think About It

1. How does Anna make her doll?
2. What do Charles, Kip, and Mitch think of Anna before she makes her doll? How do you know?
3. Anna will make an apple doll to give to a friend. Make a card to go with the doll. What will the card look like? What will it say? Draw and write your ideas.

A Day in the Life of a Seed

by Jean Groce

illustrated by Stacey Schuett

Sunflowers stand tall in the garden.
Seeds are forming in them.

In this flower, many little seeds are getting big. The pod that protects the seeds ripens. One morning it splits, and we can see the seeds. One little sunflower seed pops out. It drops down to the soil.

95

A mouse finds the seed and picks it up.

Now the seed will travel, but its trip is short.

The mouse drops it into a stream.

The seed travels in the stream past horses and tall corn. Then it gets stuck in some grass and thorns.

A rabbit hops by. It pulls up some grass
for its lunch. The grass comes up by the
roots, and the seed falls into the soil.
Its trip is over.

What will happen now? Down in the soil, the seed will sprout. Roots will form and go down into the soil. A stem will form and come up out of the soil. Leaves will form for the plant's nutrition.

The new plant will get tall in the sun.
It will have flowers that will make new seeds.
These seeds will become new plants, too. There
will be a beautiful new sunflower garden.

Think About It

1. How does the sunflower seed get to the spot where it sprouts?
2. What happens when the seed sprouts?
3. What story do you think the mouse would tell about the seed? Write the mouse's story.

Mr. Carver's Carrots

by Cassidy James   illustrated by Ellen Sasaki

The summer day was hot. The flowers were
wilted. Mr. Carver and Ben were damp and wrinkled
all over.

"I'm hungry for carrots," said Mr. Carver.

"Sounds good," said Ben. "I wish we had planted
some carrot seeds."

"What are we waiting for?" asked Mr. Carver.

Mr. Carver got some carrot seeds. Then he began to dig up the ground.

Ben knelt down. He dropped the little seeds into the soil. He put more soil on top. Now the seeds were snug beneath the dark soil.

One day a storm came. It started as a shower. Then big drops plopped down. They fell faster and faster. They sounded louder and louder.

After the storm, Ben ran outdoors. Had the seeds floated away? No! Little sprouts had popped up. Ben was proud.

A heat spell came next. The summer sun
pounded down. The carrot sprouts shimmered in
the heat.

Ben and Mr. Carver began a relay race to help
the sprouts. Ben filled buckets. Mr. Carver lugged
them around the garden.

At last! The day they had waited for came. Ben pulled on the tops of the carrots. One by one, big, beautiful carrots popped out of the ground. Ben made a tower of carrots.

Ben and Mr. Carver crunched and munched. They made a lot of noise.

Then Ben said, "Carrots are good, but you can have too many carrots!"

"You're right," said Mr. Carver. "Now I'm hungry for watermelon."

"Sounds good," said Ben. "What are we waiting for?"

Think About It

1. What do Mr. Carver and Ben do to get carrots?

2. What do they do to help the carrot plants?

3. What will Mr. Carver and Ben do with their watermelons? Draw or write your idea.

Predict Outcomes

You can predict what will happen in a story. That means that you can make a good guess about what will happen next.

You can think about story facts. You can think about what you know. You can put those things together to make a prediction about what will happen.

This chart shows how to predict what will happen in "Mr. Carver's Carrots."

Story facts +	What I know =	Prediction
Mr. Carver and Ben wanted carrots. They put carrot seeds into the soil.	Carrot plants come from seeds. Carrots come from carrot plants.	Mr. Carver and Ben will get carrots from their seeds.

Story Facts + What I already know = Prediction

Read the last page of "Mr. Carver's Carrots" again. Think about the story facts and what you know. What do you predict Mr. Carver and Ben will do?

Draw a picture for a story of your own. Write a sentence under it to tell what the story characters are doing. On the back, write what will happen next.

Ask a partner to predict what will happen next.

While the Bear SLEEPS

by Deborah Akers

illustrated by Douglas Bowles

The bear is snug in his den, but the mouse must work.
This morning, she is out looking for seeds. Last autumn she
hid some in the dirt. Today she must find them. She digs
and digs in the ground. Where are the seeds?

It is the dusky end of the day. The glowing sun has pointed out the seeds, and the mouse has found them. Now her family is fed. Her children curl up in her fur. Tomorrow the mouse must go again to get seeds. Outdoors, a storm is beginning.

The bear is snug in his den, but the bird must
work. The wind is strong this morning. The bird has
to fly very far. At last she sees something red on
some thorns in the snow. Perfect!

It is the dusky end of the day. The bird rests as the storm swirls around her. She is fed for today and will not stir until tomorrow. Then she will fly back to the thorns for more.

The bear is snug in his den, but the rabbit must work. Today he is very hungry. He cannot find any leaves. The trees are completely empty. He digs in the snow to turn up some old, brown grass. What is this in the dirt? Here is a new little sprout. There are three more!

It is the dusky end of the day. The rabbit hops home.
Today was a perfect day. He found many new plants, and
tomorrow there will be more. He knows his waiting for the
snow to melt is over.

After the snow melts, a sliver of sun will find the
bear's den. The bear will stir from his long nap and smell
the wet soil. When he knows a new day is beginning . . .

. . . the bear will get up. But look out!
He will be VERY, VERY hungry!

Think About It

1. Who has to work while the bear sleeps?

2. When does the bear sleep? When does the bear get up?

3. What do you think the bear will do when he gets up? Draw or write your idea.

The Earth in Motion

by Kana Reilly   illustrated by Melanie Barnes

You wake up.

You see the sun.

It looks as if it's coming up.

But is it?

No.

It's the earth that is in motion.

It is turning you toward the sun.

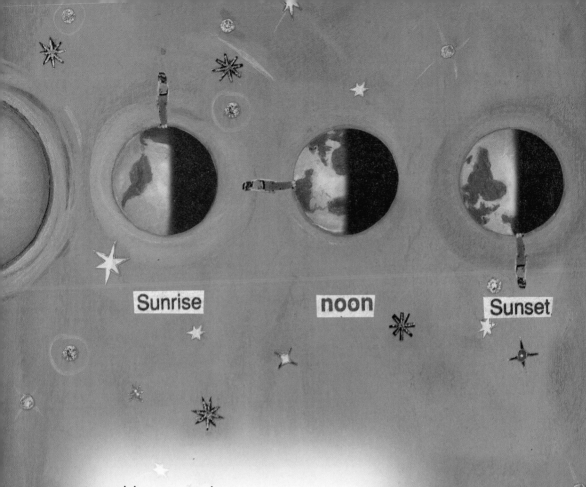

Sunrise   **noon**   **Sunset**

Hours go by.
The earth keeps turning.
All day we see the sun.
Then the light fades.
Shadows get long.
Night comes.

Here is an experiment you can do.

It will show what makes day and night.

Pull the shade to make it dark.

Get a lamp.

Like the sun, the lamp gives light.

Take a ball.

Like the earth, the ball is round.

Make a spot on the ball.

Imagine that the spot is you.

Spin the ball.
Make it turn as the earth does.
Watch the spot.
First it is in the light.
You have day.

Turn the ball again.
Now the spot is in a shadow.
You have night.

Turn some more.
The spot comes out of the shadow.
You come back to the light again.

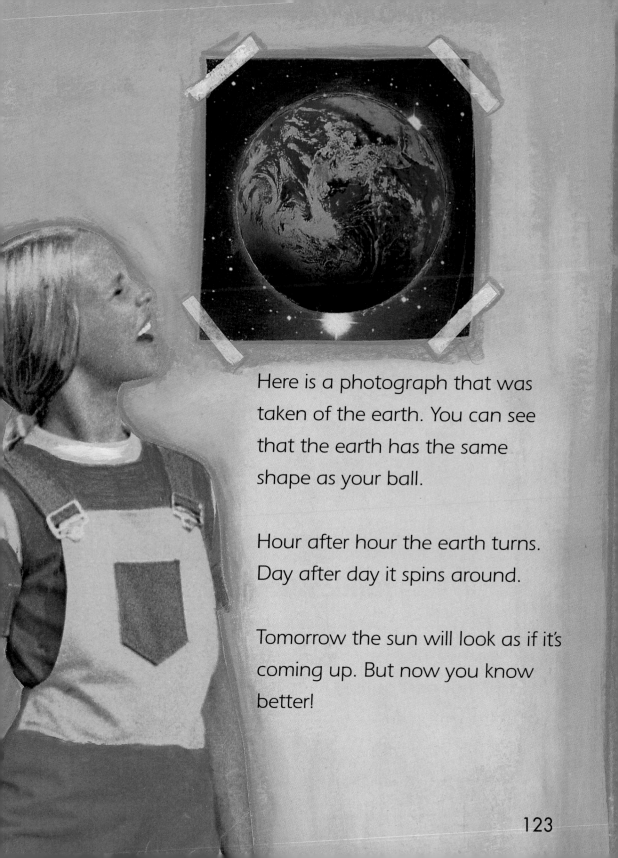

Here is a photograph that was taken of the earth. You can see that the earth has the same shape as your ball.

Hour after hour the earth turns. Day after day it spins around.

Tomorrow the sun will look as if it's coming up. But now you know better!

Think About It

1. What is happening when we see the sun come up?

2. What part of the day is it when our part of earth turns away from the sun?

3. Draw a picture of your favorite part of the day. Show where the sun is.

124

Important Details

Story details are bits of information. They answer *who, what, where, when, how,* and *why* questions. Some story details are very important. Other story details tell more about the important details.

In the middle of this web, you can see an important detail from "The Earth in Motion." Other details tell more about that important detail.

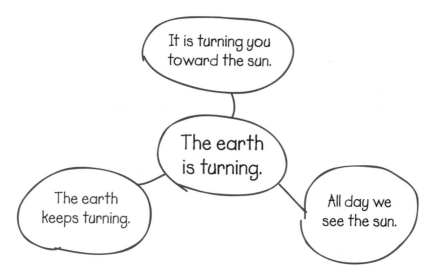

Find another sentence from "The Earth in Motion" that tells a detail about the earth turning.

Now write about the sun. Draw a web to show your plan. In the middle circle, write your most important detail. Write other details in the rest of the circles.

The NOT-So-Boring Night

by Kathryn Corbett

illustrated by Wong Herbert Yee

It was a hot night at our summer cabin by the lake. Rose and I were on the porch, playing her fishing game. Mom said, "Jerome, thanks for playing with Rose."

I said, "This game is for little kids. This will be a boring night."

"Maybe not," Mom said. "You like to fish."

"This is not fishing," I said.

I was glad when our Doberman, Duke, barked to go for a walk. I could use a walk myself. "All right, Duke," I said to him. To Mom and Rose I said, "Excuse me. I'll be right back."

"Don't go too close to the lake," Mom called after me.

"No, Mom," I called back, and Duke and I ran off.

"Thanks, Duke!" I said. "That game is so boring. I was starting to doze off, and Rose gets mad when I snore!"

We went down to the cove. I hummed a tune as Duke dug a hole. Then I froze. Someone was by the dunes! I ducked down next to Duke.

It was the farmer we get eggs from for our lunches. Rose and I have fun throwing corn to his chickens.

I supposed it made sense that the farmer would fish here. I'd just never seen him off the farm. But something was very odd. He was throwing back all the fish he got!

Duke and I walked over to the dunes. "I see you're getting lots of fish," I said.

"Oh, yes," the farmer said. "I do very well with this pole." He held it out for me to look at.

I was amazed to see that he was fishing with a magnet!

He swung the pole again and got one more fish. Something was odd about the fish, too. It was red, and it had a number on it! The farmer jotted something in a little notepad. Then he tossed the fish back into the lake.

"Excuse me," I asked him, "but why are you throwing them all back? What are you putting in your notepad?"

"Oh," he said, "that's my score. I like fishing, but I don't like to take the fish out of the water. So I just make a game of it."

He was adding up his score when I felt a sharp poke.

"Jerome! You're starting to snore," Rose said. I woke up with a plastic fish dangling over my nose. The fish was red, and it had a number on it. Rose giggled.

"Poor Jerome is bored," Mom said. "Come on, you two. Let's walk to the store before it closes and get cones." Rose clapped her hands.

"Okay," I said, "but let's play some more before bed. I like this game better than fishing now."

Think About It

1. What happens when Jerome plays a game with Rose?

2. Why does Jerome think it was not a boring night after all?

3. Make a list of other games you think Jerome might enjoy.

The Matador and Me

by Kathryn Corbett
illustrated by Keiko Motoyama

When vacation time comes,
I go west on a train
    To visit Aunt Clementine's
ranch on the plain.
    My parents have told me so often that I'm
working my imagination overtime.
    "Don't let it be captured—relax, let it rest.
Use your good manners. Behave your best."

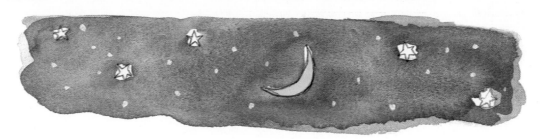

Aunt Clementine's not big
on manners and rules—
    She thinks that they're fine
for parents and schools.
    No forks by our campfire,
just fingers instead,
    And if we're not tired, we
don't go to bed.
    The one thing that's missing
is someone my size
    To think up new games
with. But this year—surprise!

When I saddled my horse and rode over next door
A big kid was there dressed like a matador!
He was up on a visit from Mexico
Where bulls chase red capes and matadors go
To work in fine clothes that glitter and shine,
But that kind of work would never be mine!

My new pal was glum. He just didn't know
How to get bulls to turn where invited to go.
He'd swing his cape left and the bull would go right.
"At this rate," he said, "we'd be there all night."
"I'll help you," I said. We tied horns to my hat.
Then he waved his red shirt, and I ran after that.

I plowed into him, and down he went, flat
On his back in the mud, and that was that.
The cowboys lined up by the barbed wire howled.
My matador friend just sat there and growled,
"I give up. Those old bulls will think I'm a joke.
They won't see a matador—just a slowpoke."

I said, "Maybe this matador job's not for you.
There must be some other work you can do."
"Like what?" asked my friend as I helped him to stand.
"Well, there's farmer and rancher and even cowhand."
"You're right," he said. Then he held out his hand.
"I'd rather go home and just farm the land."

My parents don't think my story is true,
So I'll save it for school and ask—do you?

Think About It

1. What does the girl do on her vacation?
2. Do you think the big kid has been working on his matador skills very long? Why or why not?
3. If the girl wrote a letter to her parents, what would she say?

Context Clues for Word Meaning

What can you do when you read a word you don't know? Sometimes story pictures can tell you what the word means. Sometimes other words and sentences can help you understand the word.

Reread page 136 from "The Matador and Me." Then look at the picture. It helps you know what the word *matador* means.

You could read this sentence in a story. A picture could help you understand what the word *pinto* means.

The pinto ran fast.

Pick one of the words in the box. Find out what the word means. Then write a sentence with that word. Draw a picture to go with your sentence.

lasso wrangler bronco

Show your sentence and picture to a partner. Can your partner tell what the word means?

Mr. Whiskers

by Meish Goldish
illustrated by Laura Ovresat

Hi! I'm Neal. This is Mr. Whiskers, my seal friend. His home is in the sea. You can see my home on the beach.

Mr. Whiskers and I meet here at the beach each weekend. He teaches me about his friends in the ocean. I have a lot of information about seals now.

Mr. Whiskers seems to know all the seals in the ocean. He knows most of the whales, too. He's glad that the sea is so big. If he were in a little pond, he wouldn't have so many friends to greet!

Mr. Whiskers is a good swimmer. He uses his flippers forcibly to reach his top speed. I can swim fast, but not that fast!

Mr. Whiskers and his seal friends swim fast and far. See this map? The seals swam from here to here and didn't get lost. Seals don't need a map!

One time we had a swimming contest to see which seal could swim the fastest. The seals swam out where the sea is deep. I ran along the beach. At first a big seal was in the lead. Then the leader was Mr. Whiskers. He beat all the seals. He was the winner!

Can you see how Mr. Whiskers got his name? Look at his cheeks. His whiskers help him feel around in the water. They help him find a good meal to eat!

Mr. Whiskers has lots of sharp teeth. He uses them to feast on fish. What a treat for him!

Mr. Whiskers keeps himself very neat. When he comes out of the water, he is so sleek! He would make a very clean pet. But seals can't walk well on land. Their back feet are flippers, too.

Sometimes I wish I were a seal. Swimming all the time would keep me clean. I would never need to take a bath. Now that would be a real treat!

Mom and Dad have never seen Mr. Whiskers. I tell them the details about what we do each weekend.

Dad says, "Sounds like fun, Neal."

Mom says, "How sweet, dear. Now go to sleep."

I know this means they think Mr. Whiskers is not real. They think I see him in my dreams.

This disappoints me a little. I tell them, "Mr. Whiskers is real!"

They just smile. When Mr. Whiskers hears about this, he smiles too. And then, so do I!

Think About It

1. What are two things the boy has learned about seals?

2. Why do the boy's parents think Mr. Whiskers is just something their son dreams about?

3. Draw a picture of Mr. Whiskers with some of his ocean friends. Label each kind of animal you draw.

IF A DINOSAUR WENT TO THE VET

BY CHEYENNE CISCO
ILLUSTRATED BY ELDON DOTY

Gail liked to play vet.
One day, a stray roamed
in to see Dr. Gail.
It was not a stray dog.
It was not a stray cat.
This stray was different.
Very different!
It was a stray dinosaur!

150

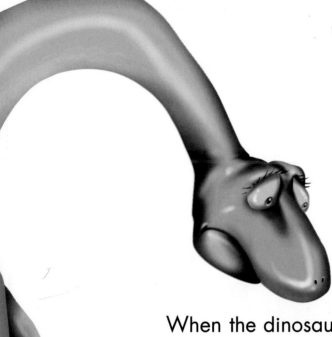

Dr. Gail,
Veterinarian

When the dinosaur reached Dr. Gail, it came to a halt.

"I'm Fay," the dinosaur said. "May I come in?"

Dr. Gail looked up–way, way up! "Okay," she said, "but all dinosaurs are extinct!"

"I can't imagine why you think that!" Fay exclaimed. "I am very much alive, but now I have a pain. If you don't help me, I may faint!"

"You feel faint?" Dr. Gail asked. "I can't imagine why. I don't see any problem here."

"I feel faint from the pain in my tail," Fay explained.

"Have courage, Fay," said Dr. Gail. "Wait right here, okay?"

Dr. Gail walked over to Fay's tail.

"Is this where the pain is?" asked Dr. Gail.

"Probably," said Fay. "It's so far away. I can't tell."

"Your tail hit that gate very hard. It's probably sprained," said Dr. Gail.

"Imagine that!" Fay exclaimed. Just then Fay shifted, and her tail knocked Dr. Gail down.

"Ow!" yelled Dr. Gail. "Now I'VE got a sprain!"

"I'm so sorry, Dr. Gail!" said Fay.
"Are you okay?"

"I'm fine," said Dr. Gail.
"Now rub this on your tail
four times a day. Stay out
of the rain, and no wagging!"

"Okay," said Fay. "You're
such a good vet! I'll tell the herd."

"A herd of dinosaurs!"
said Dr. Gail to herself.
"Imagine that!"

Gail still likes to play
vet, and strays still roam
in to see her. Just one
thing is different now...

Think About It

1. What does Dr. Gail do to help Fay the dinosaur?

2. Does Dr. Gail want to treat a herd of dinosaurs? How can you tell?

3. What do you think Fay might say when she gets back to her herd? Write Fay's speech.

Reality and Fantasy

Some stories tell about things that could not happen in real life. These stories are make-believe, or fantasy.

This chart tells about some of the make-believe things in "If a Dinosaur Went to the Vet." It also tells what could take place in a real-life story.

Make-Believe Story	Real-Life Story
"I'm Fay," the dinosaur said.	Jeb's dog barked.
"Rub this on your tail," said Dr. Gail.	"Rub this on your dog's paw," said Dr. Clark to Jeb.
"Okay," said Fay. "You're such a good vet."	"Okay," said Jeb. "You're such a good vet."

You might read a story about a cat who grows corn and beans. Would that be a make-believe story or a real-life story? How do you know?

Draw pictures for two stories. In one picture, show what could happen in a make-believe story. In the other, show what could happen in a real-life story. Ask a partner to tell which picture is from a make-believe story.

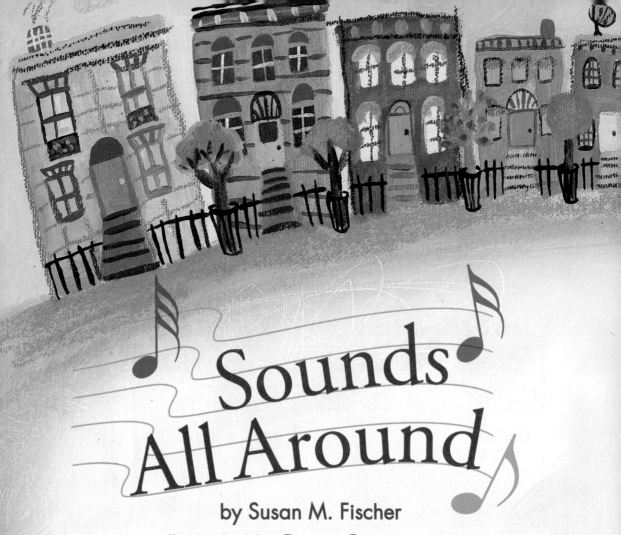

Sounds All Around

by Susan M. Fischer

illustrated by Donna Ingemanson

Jules was the first to notice that Mrs. Lee was not home. He asked Mr. Jones where she was.

"Mrs. Lee is sick. She went to the hospital," said Mr. Jones. "I hope she will not be there long."

Jules was sad. He liked seeing Mrs. Lee when he walked home from school. She loved to sit and watch the crowd go by.

Jules walked down the sidewalk. Mr. Jones was making his chalk art on it. Kids were playing games. Mrs. Peck was selling fruit from her cart. Sue was playing a cool tune on her flute. A dump truck went rushing by.

Then it started to rain. The chalk drawings began to run. Jules listened to the noisy rain. He was thinking hard. Before long, he had a plan.

In the morning there was still a haze from the
rainstorm. Jules went with his mom to see Mrs. Lee.
He had a big bag in his arms.

Mrs. Lee looked a little pale. A nurse fussed
by her bed. When the nurse left, Jules gave
Mrs. Lee a hug. She asked what was in his bag.

Jules pulled out some fruit from Mrs. Peck. All the children had made drawings for her. Mr. Jones sent some chalk so Mrs. Lee could make drawings, too.

Mrs. Lee admired her presents. "Thank you, Jules. I miss watching the crowd on the sidewalk. These will keep me from feeling homesick."

Then Jules pulled out the coolest present of all.

He pressed the button on his tape player.
The tape played a sound that went *thup,
thup, thup.*

"Do you know what that is?" asked Jules.
"I'll give you a clue. It's something you
can eat."

"It sounds like fruit dropping into a bag,"
said Mrs. Lee.

"Right! It's this fruit from Mrs. Peck!" said
Jules. "Now, what is this?" There was a
whap-thump, whap-thump.

Mrs. Lee had to think. "It's the kids jumping rope!"

Next there was a loud *bam-bam-zoom*.

"That's a truck," she said.

Then the tape played a sweet tune. Mrs. Lee smiled. "That must be Sue!" Jules stood up and mimicked Sue playing the flute.

When the song was over, Mrs. Lee clapped. "Thank you, Jules!" she said. "I was feeling blue. Now I feel as if I'm right there in the crowd."

The tape played one more sound. It was a light noise at first, but then it got louder.

"Rain!" Mrs. Lee said. They all listened to the cool sound of rain on the sidewalk.

Mrs. Lee picked up the chalk. She drew a rainbow. Then she put some words under it. *Thank you, my friends. I can't wait to see you all again!*

Think About It

1. How does Jules cheer up Mrs. Lee during her stay in the hospital?

2. How do you think Jules is able to get people in the neighborhood to help with Mrs. Lee's surprise?

3. Draw a picture of Jules taping another neighborhood sound to take to Mrs. Lee. Write a sentence telling how Jules got the idea of taping sounds.

THE LITTLE LIGHTHOUSE

By Kaye Gager

Illustrated by Jui Ishida

Today is a sad day for my family and me. We are going to a new home. We listen for a storm, but the water is still. Then we get into the boat and quietly float away. The little lighthouse is left all alone.

I watch the light glow in the mist. I am sorry to leave the little lighthouse that was my home.

I will miss helping look for boats lost in the fog. Our family kept the light on, night and day, for boats to see.

"The lighthouse will miss us," I say.

My family all agree.

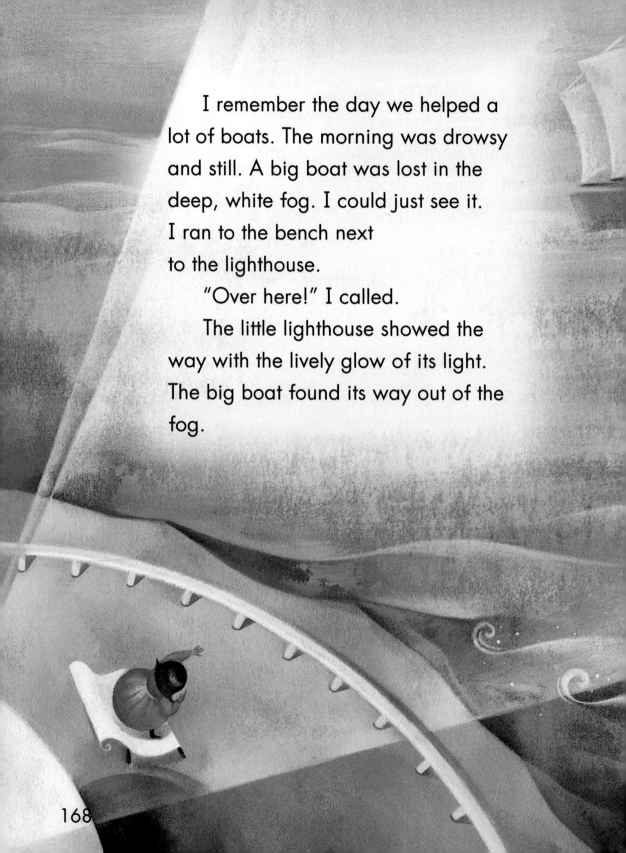

I remember the day we helped a lot of boats. The morning was drowsy and still. A big boat was lost in the deep, white fog. I could just see it. I ran to the bench next to the lighthouse.

"Over here!" I called.

The little lighthouse showed the way with the lively glow of its light. The big boat found its way out of the fog.

Then a little boat sailed too close to the shore. It was about to hit the rocks because it couldn't see in the fog.

"Stay away!" I shouted. "You're too close to the rocks!" With a gentle roar of its horn, the lighthouse agreed.

The little boat turned around and sailed away safely.

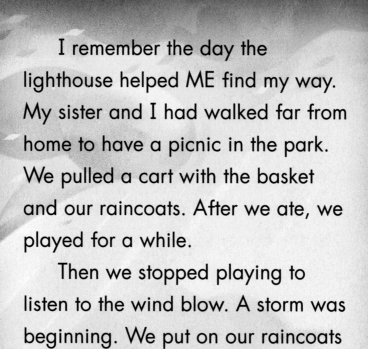

I remember the day the
lighthouse helped ME find my way.
My sister and I had walked far from
home to have a picnic in the park.
We pulled a cart with the basket
and our raincoats. After we ate, we
played for a while.

Then we stopped playing to
listen to the wind blow. A storm was
beginning. We put on our raincoats
and started for home.

The rain came down harder and harder. Our feet were getting soaked. A white mist floated low over the trees, and we couldn't see the road. We were lost.

The thunder roared, but then we could hear a different roar. It was our own little lighthouse! Its horn called out to us again and again. We listened and followed the sound until we found our way home.

Now a new family will come to the lighthouse. They will watch for lost boats. They will keep the light on, night and day. Maybe there will be a new girl to help look for lost boats. Maybe she will stand on the bench and call to them the way I did.

I hope the new family will love the little lighthouse, too. I know that my sister and I will listen to it in our dreams.

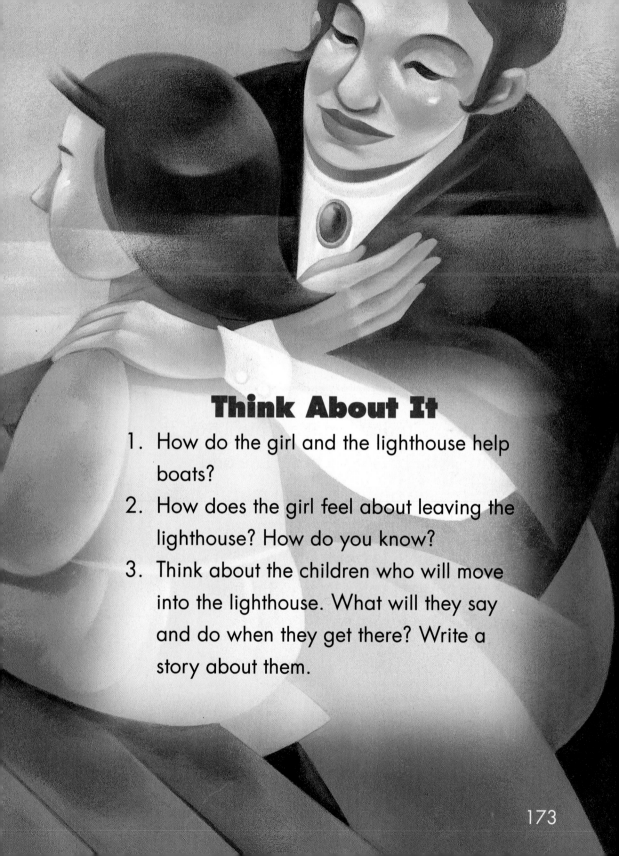

Think About It

1. How do the girl and the lighthouse help boats?

2. How does the girl feel about leaving the lighthouse? How do you know?

3. Think about the children who will move into the lighthouse. What will they say and do when they get there? Write a story about them.

A Secret Place

by Linda Olivares

illustrated by Brad Weinman

Characters	
Narrator	Jo
Lee	Mom

Narrator: Today is not a typical day. It's a snow day, so there is no school. Lee and Jo played outside in the cold all morning. Now they have come in for lunch.

Jo: Oh, no! The blocks have been knocked over. What caused this? Wags, did you run wild in here while we were out?

174

Lee: What's going on? One of my cars is missing, too.

Lee: Jo, did you take my car? I bet you did. I bet it's in your secret hiding place.

Jo: Don't blame me! I didn't take your old car. Maybe you have my missing blocks. Maybe you put them in *your* secret hiding place.

Jo and Lee: Mom!!!

Mom: No one stole anything! You can find the missing objects. Just think for a bit, and then look around. It will be easy to spot a small, shiny car. Those blocks will be hard to miss. Look for clues.

Jo: Okay. I'll be the chief.

Lee: I'll be the helper. Look! Wags wants to be a helper, too.

Mom: You make a good team! Look behind things and under things. I'll be in the den if you need me.

Narrator: Mom comes back in. She looks confused.

Mom: Now I have a missing object, too. The clasp on my key ring broke, and I can't find my car key.

Jo: We'll look for clues, Mom.

Lee: A shiny gold key will be easy to spot.

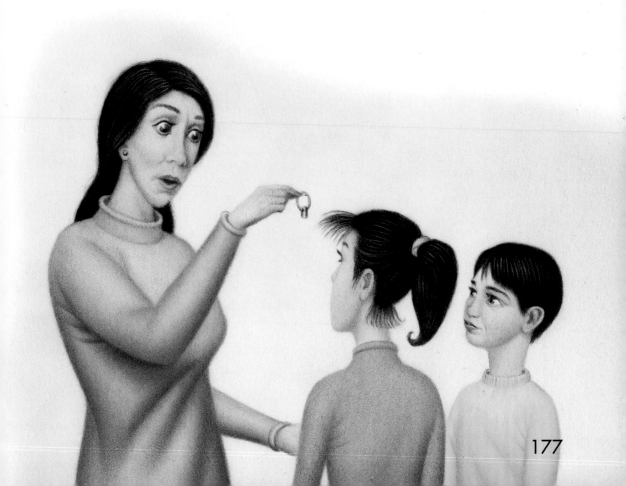

Narrator: Everyone leaves the room but Wags. He goes back to sit on his bed.

Think About It

1. Why can't Lee and Jo find the missing blocks, car, and key?

2. How do Lee and Jo feel when they find out where the missing objects are? How do you know?

3. Imagine that Wags can talk. What will he say about the missing objects and how they were found? Write a story for Wags to tell.

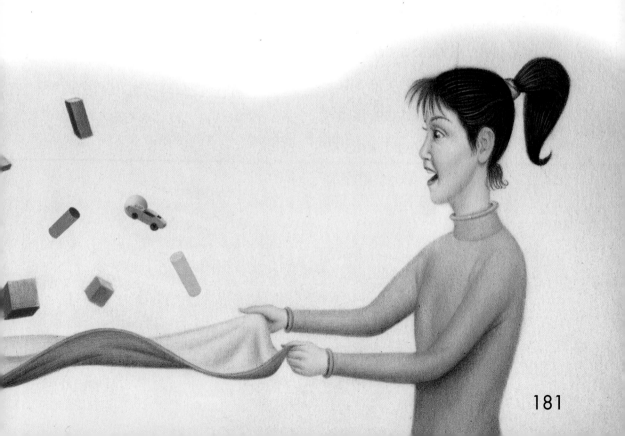

Hello from Here

by Deborah Eaton

illustrated by Julia Gorton

My street is just like most streets. The houses sit side by side. Kids play in the yards.

My house is the sky-blue one. The one next to it belongs to Ms. Pryor, the town clerk. Mr. Clyde's house is at the very end of the street.

Mr. Clyde is my friend, and I know why. He likes kids!

This July, all the kids on the street got a surprise! Mail started to pour into our mailboxes.

July 1
Surprise!
Hi from the sky! My oh my! I've been waiting for years to try sky diving. It feels like flying!
Wish you were here.

Who would send us these cards, and why? Who would know our addresses?

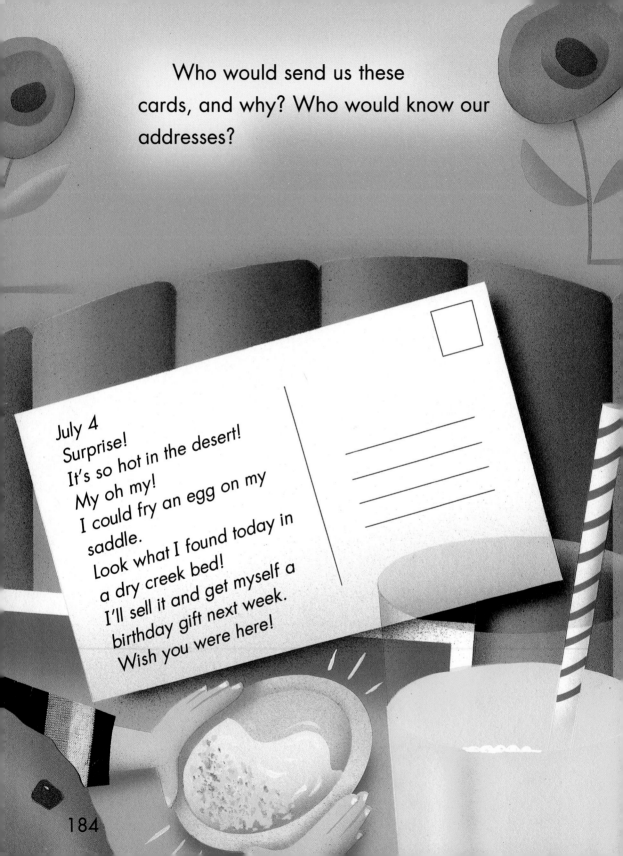

July 4
Surprise!
It's so hot in the desert!
My oh my!
I could fry an egg on my saddle.
Look what I found today in a dry creek bed!
I'll sell it and get myself a birthday gift next week.
Wish you were here!

I had to find out who it was. I tried
to think like a spy. I looked for clues. Then
I realized there were no stamps on the
cards! They were not coming on our mail
route.

The next morning I hid by our
mailbox and waited. Before long a grown
person came along, acting sneaky. When he
stopped by our mailbox, I jumped up.

"Got you!" I yelled.

"My oh my!" cried Mr. Clyde.
He had a stack of cards in one hand.
He was about to drop one into the mailbox.
"Mr. Clyde!" I exclaimed. "The cards
are fun, but why did you do this?"

"I don't have any grandchildren," he
said. "So all of you are like grandchildren
to me. It was fun to give you cards and
clues. You found out my secret!"

Then it was my turn. I sent cards to all the kids
on the street.

You're Invited

You're Invited

You're Invited

You're Invited

You're Invited

You're Invited

You're Invited

July 10
Surprise!
You are invited to a party
in honor of Mr. Clyde's
birthday. We will play
games and fly kites! It will
be next Saturday at two.
Don't miss the party of
all parties!
See you there!

Myles

Think About It

1. How does Mr. Clyde feel about the kids on the street? What does he do for them?

2. After talking to Mr. Clyde, how does Myles feel about him? How do you know?

3. After the party, Mr. Clyde will send a postcard to Myles. What will he say? Draw a picture for the postcard, too.

Summarize

A summary tells what a story is about. It tells only the most important things that happen in the story. It tells them in story order, but the summary is shorter than the story.

Read the sentences in the box. They form a summary of "Hello from Here."

> **My friends and I got postcards.**
>
> **We did not know who sent the postcards.**
>
> **I saw Mr. Clyde put one of the cards in a mailbox.**
>
> **Mr. Clyde said we were like his grandchildren.**
>
> **I planned a birthday party for Mr. Clyde.**

Now read these sentences. Tell why they are not part of the story summary.

> **Mr. Clyde's house is on my street.**
>
> **Mr. Clyde said, "My oh my."**
>
> **The kids will fly kites at the party.**

Think about another story you have read. What are the most important things that happen? Write a summary of the story, or give one aloud.

The Music Maker

by Sydnie Meltzer Kleinhenz

illustrated by Roberta Ludlow

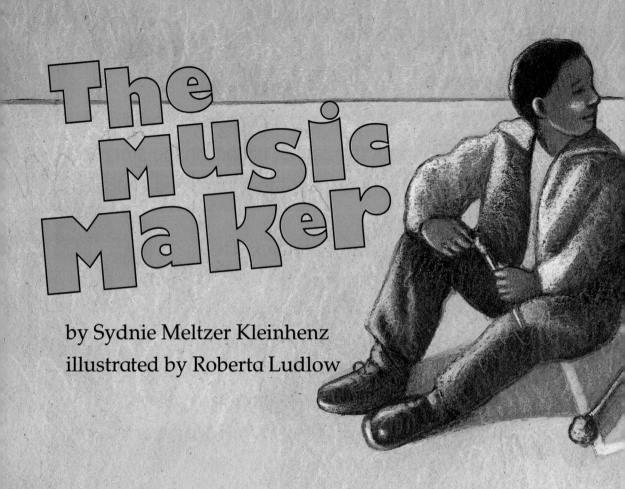

Wherever Dwight went, his drumsticks went, too. He tapped on anything he could find. He liked to try new ways to make his rhythms sound better.

Dwight spotted some rubber bands on the playground. He wound them around the ends of two sticks. He twisted them into tight rubber balls. Then he used them to beat a rhythm on his boxes.

"What are you doing?" Jon asked.

"I'm trying to get the right sound," Dwight answered. He tapped on the plastic bucket.

"You need good drumsticks to make a good sound," Jon said. "Those look mighty bad to me."

"They just aren't right for this bucket drum," Dwight said. "Maybe I'll try them on something else."

Dwight spotted a garbage can on the playground. He drummed on the garbage can's lid. BANG-BANG-BANG! The loud sound startled the children nearby. They put their hands over their ears. Jon's friend Linda appeared at his side.

"What are you doing, Dwight?" she asked. "You gave me such a fright!"

"I'm working on the notes of my music," Dwight answered. "I'm going to play 'The Star-Spangled Banner' at the baseball game Saturday night."

Linda sighed. "You must mean you'll drum out the beat," she said. "You can't play the notes of 'The Star-Spangled Banner' on a drum."

Jon giggled. "You need a trumpet or a flute to play real music," he said. He imitated a trumpet player.

"MY drum CAN make real music," Dwight answered. "Come over to my house after school, and I'll show you."

194

Dwight's dad had a workshop behind the house. Jon and Linda watched him heat a big steel can. He hammered shapes into the top of it and then put it in water. This created clouds of steam. When he pulled it out of the water, he tapped on the shapes. To Jon and Linda's surprise, notes sounded. "That drum does make music!" said Jon.

On Saturday night, Jon and Linda went to the
baseball game. Before the game began, the
conductor lifted his arms high. All the fans got up.
Then the band started playing "The Star-Spangled
Banner." Dwight delighted the crowd as he made
music on his steel drum.

Think About It

1. What can Dwight do on his drum that most drummers cannot do?
2. How does Dwight feel about the drums his dad makes? How do you know?
3. Do you think Dwight's dad sells the drums he makes? Write an advertisement for a steel drum.

Rodeo!

by Robert Newell

Howdy, partner!
Is a ten-gallon hat just
your style? Do you wish
you were handy with a
rope? Would you trade
your shiny bike for a
dappled pony?
Really?
Well then, today is
your lucky day. Welcome
to an exhibition of style
and skill.
Welcome to the rodeo!

Hang on, Cowboy!

Could you ride this horse for 8 seconds? Bronc riders have to, and they hold on with only one hand. To them, 8 seconds can be a very long time!

Many of the riders in small rodeos work on a ranch. They can practice daily. Even so, many of them quickly hit the dirt. Ouch! This muddy cowboy tried his best. Now he's seeing the landscape close up. Better luck next time!

You have to be speedy for this event. You must practice, practice, practice. Roping is pretty tricky. This cowgirl may have thrown her rope thousands of times! Her pony helps her. It backs up to keep the rope tight. The cowgirl's turn is over in less than 60 seconds. Good work!

Riding a bull is a risky business. This one looks really angry. Style is not very important here. You just have to hang on!

They're silly and they're funny-looking,
but clowns are important to rodeo families.
Safety is their job. When riders fall, the
clowns keep the horse or bull away from
them. It's dirty, dusty work, but somebody
has to do it.

The rodeo is more than 100 years old. July 4, America's birthday, is the rodeo's birthday, too. So come on, partner! Let's wish the rodeo a happy birthday!

Think About It

1. Name three rodeo events cowboys and cowgirls can take part in.

2. How do you think rodeo riders feel about rodeo clowns? Why?

3. Imagine that a rodeo is coming to your town. Make a poster for the rodeo. Use drawings and words in your poster.

Main Idea

Most paragraphs in a story have a **main idea** and **important details.** The main idea is what the paragraph is mostly about. The important details tell more about the main idea.

Read this paragraph from "Rodeo!" Which sentence tells the main idea of the paragraph? What are the important details?

Riding a bull is a risky business. This one looks really angry. Style is not very important here. You just have to hang on!

Write your own paragraph about a game you like. Finish the sentence below to tell your main idea. Then add two or three sentences to your paragraph. Tell what makes the game fun.

Playing _____ is fun.

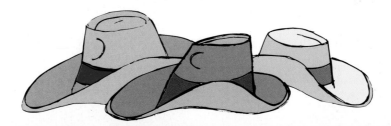

Zelda
Moves to the Desert

by Linda Lott

illustrated by Tim Bowers

Each night, Zelda the bat went flying. She worked hard to find food. She ate bug after bug.

One morning, as Zelda returned home, a gentle rain was falling. Zelda was tired and wet when she reached her cozy cave. She folded her wings. The little creek sang to her as she drifted off to sleep.

As Zelda slept, the rain fell harder and the creek got bigger. The water rose higher, right up to the ledge of her cozy cave.

When night came, Zelda woke up. The water had begun to come in. Her home would soon be flooded. Zelda peeked over the edge of the ledge. She dropped a rock into the water and it sank far down. The water was deep!

The creek was rushing past the cave very quickly. Zelda watched a bottle drift past. Then some little mice floated by in a bowl. They were using it as a boat. "You'd better find a new home, Zelda!" the mice shouted.

Zelda sighed. She realized that the mice were right. "My cave is not cozy anymore," she said to herself. "It is not even safe. I must find a new home that is safe and dry."

Giant clouds were still looming when
Zelda launched herself from the ledge. First
she flapped her way into the forest.

"It's too damp in here!" said Zelda.
"This is not a good home for me."

Next Zelda fluttered out over the sea.
She looked down at a fleet of boats bobbing
on the waves. They had sails of bright colors.

"The sailboats on the dark sea look like
little gems on black velvet," said Zelda. "But
the sea is not a good home for me. It's much
too wet!"

210

Zelda kept on flying as the sun started to rise over the horizon. Suddenly she spotted sand below. She realized she was over the desert.

"The desert is very dry," Zelda said. "I think I have found just the right spot for me!"

As morning came, Zelda slid under a ledge in a tiny cave. She slept well in her dry, cozy new home.

Think About It

1. Why does Zelda leave her cave? Why does she move to the desert?
2. Would Zelda like to have a home by a lake? How do you know?
3. How will Zelda feel when she wakes up in her new desert home? What will she do? Write your ideas.

Cause and Effect

Think about "Zelda Moves to the Desert." Why does Zelda go out to find a new home? Look at the chart. Read the sentences about the story.

Cause ➞	Effect
The creek floods Zelda's cave.	She must find a new home that is dry.

The first sentence tells you that the creek floods Zelda's cave. This is the **cause.** It tells you **why** something happens.

The second sentence tells you that Zelda must find a new home that is dry. This is the **effect.** It tells you **what** happens because of something else.

Look at this picture. Think about what is happening. Write one sentence that tells the cause. Write another sentence that tells the effect.

When You Visit Relatives

by Hector Morales
illustrated by Sandra Shap

I'll see you soon, Aunt Mabel.

You're coming tomorrow!?!

Call First

If you want to visit your relatives, don't forget to call them first. Let them know your travel plans. They will have to get ready for company. Pick out a nice present to take to them.

Ask a Companion to Join You

Instead of traveling alone, you might invite a friend to come along. First you should ask your relatives if it's okay. Don't make it a surprise!

Get Out Those Wheels

How will you get there? Biking is fine if it's not far and the weather is good. Avoid traffic. Travel on safe roads.

Don't forget to take along some snacks. You will probably get hungry.

Get Out That Luggage

Pack sturdy clothes and toys—enough for several days. Travel light so you don't put too much on your bicycle.

Don't let bad weather spoil your trip. Remember to take your raincoat. Dry travelers are happy travelers.

Follow the Rules

Handle your own luggage.

Wipe your feet on the mat.

Keep your cassette player turned low.

Don't jump on the bed.

Don't eat in bed.

Don't make a lot of noise.

DON'T STAY TOO LONG!

Help Out

Don't just sit around. Offer to help with the chores.

Make your bed each day. Pick up your toys. Make lunches for everyone. Wash the dishes, too. Your relatives will be happy to have your help.

Say Thank You

Tell your relatives what a good time you had. Thank them for having you. Then invite them to visit you soon.

Make a point of writing a thank-you note when you get home. Your relatives will remember your visit with joy!

Dear Relatives,
Thank you for
everything. I am
sorry we broke
Your

Think About It

1. When you plan to visit relatives, what should you do first? What are two things you should do so you won't annoy your relatives?

2. Why is it a good choice to take a raincoat on a trip?

3. After Ernest and his friend leave, his relatives talk about his visit. Draw a cartoon of the relatives. Write sentences to show what they say.

If I Could FLY

by Deborah Akers

illustrated by Cathy Diefendorf

"Where would you go if you could fly?" Luke asked June and Sally.

"We *can't* fly," said June.

"If we could, I would take off like a plane," said Luke. "I would glide like a bird. I would soar over rain clouds."

"Then where would you go?" asked Sally.

Luke said, "I would fly to the city. I've never, ever been to a big city."

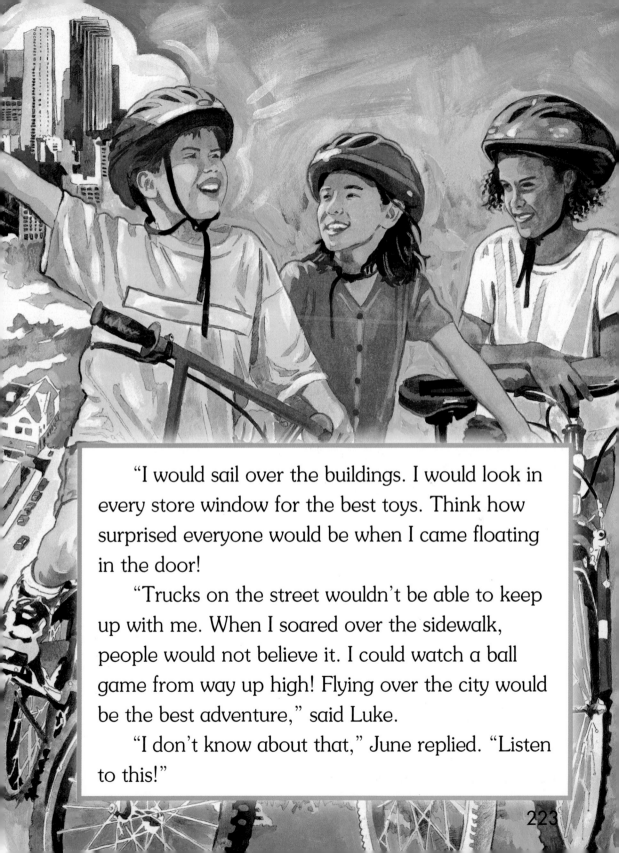

"I would sail over the buildings. I would look in every store window for the best toys. Think how surprised everyone would be when I came floating in the door!

"Trucks on the street wouldn't be able to keep up with me. When I soared over the sidewalk, people would not believe it. I could watch a ball game from way up high! Flying over the city would be the best adventure," said Luke.

"I don't know about that," June replied. "Listen to this!"

"If I could fly, I would travel far away. I would join a flock of birds down at the harbor. We would go swooping across the wide blue sea.

"I would find a country where people love to play. I'd watch them have fun all day. When they saw me fly, they would beg me to show them how.

224

"Soon everyone would know how to fly. Then we would have a big party in the sky! We would eat cake above the trees. We would dance on the clouds. Now THAT would be the best adventure," said June.

Sally shook her head. "Oh, I don't know," she said.

Luke and June asked, "Well, what would you do, Sally?"

Sally said, "Your adventures would be lots of fun. But if I could fly, I would do something different. I would visit my grandma. Last fall she moved far away, and I miss her so much!

"I would fly to the top of her building. I would look in her window. She would be so surprised! She would give me a big hug. Then she would cook me the best meal in the world.

"After we ate, we could take a walk. Grandma lives near the sea now. Maybe we could go fishing. We could look for whales, too!

"We could watch the sun go down. Then I would show Grandma how I've learned to read. I could read from my book until she fell asleep."

Sally said, "I guess that doesn't sound like a big adventure to you, but it would be the best one for me!"

Think About It

1. Where would Luke, June, and Sally go if they could fly?

2. How does Sally feel about her grandma? How do you know?

3. Which adventure would you like best— Luke's, June's, or Sally's? What makes that adventure best? Write about your ideas.

Word Endings

Knowing about word parts can help you read new words. In some words, you might see a suffix. A **suffix** is a word ending that has its own meaning. These are three suffixes you might find when you read.

-ly -ful -ness

Read these sentences about "If I Could Fly." What suffix can you find in each sentence?

Luke wants to fly **quickly**.

June will be **cheerful** when she flies.

Sally misses her grandma's **kindness**.

Now read these sentences. In each sentence, find the word with a suffix. What is the suffix?

Sally rode slowly home on her bike.

She was thinking about her grandma's goodness.

Grandma was always so helpful.

Make your own words with suffixes. Add *-ly, -ful*, or *-ness* to the words *friend, joy,* and *dark.* Then write a sentence with that word.

friend joy dark

AN AMAZING FEAT

by Susan M. Fischer

illustrated by Bryn Barnard

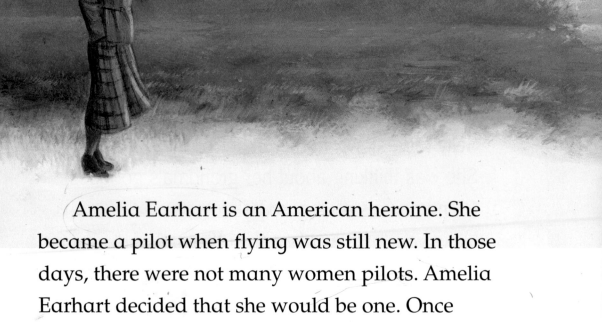

Amelia Earhart is an American heroine. She
became a pilot when flying was still new. In those
days, there were not many women pilots. Amelia
Earhart decided that she would be one. Once
Amelia decided something, she would not give up.
She refused to sit at home. She wanted to show
that women could do more.

Amelia was eleven when she first came upon an airplane at a fair. That was the place where she fell in love with flying.

When Amelia was a teenager, a war started, and she helped as a nurse. She watched the pilots and listened to the plane engines roar. After the war she decided she wanted to fly herself.

Amelia had some money from her grandmother. This let her take the flying lessons she wanted. She was even able to get her own plane, the *Friendship*. In it she flew higher than any woman had flown.

Soon flying was the center of Amelia's life. She flew to places all over the world. She was the first woman to fly across the Atlantic alone. What an amazing feat! Later she set new records for speed and distance.

Amelia Earhart became well-known around the world. Spectators came to cheer when she took off and landed. Amelia thanked the people of each city for their hospitality.

Amelia had one more dream. It would be an even more amazing feat. She wanted to fly all the way around the world!

In 1937, when she was forty years old, she got her chance. This time she would take her friend Fred Noonan. A partner would add weight but would be needed on such a long trip.

234

Together they filled the tanks with gasoline and checked the engines. As they took off, spectators stood and watched with pride and hope.

The plane had flown most of the way when it ran out of fuel. Amelia Earhart, her partner, and her plane disappeared. Hundreds of people have looked for them ever since. The plane has never been found.

Amelia Earhart said of her flying, "The dreams of long ago had come true." She showed everyone that to live your dream, you must never give up. Amelia Earhart is a heroine to celebrate.

Think About It

1. Why do we think of Amelia Earhart as a heroine?

2. Why would a flying partner be helpful on a long trip?

3. You are a newspaper reporter in 1937. Write a news story about Amelia Earhart's last plane trip.

Flying Pigs

SPACE TRIP

by Caren B. Stelson
illustrated by
Wayne Vincent

Hello, everyone! I'm Paula Planet of Universe
Space Trips. I'll be your space guide. Is everyone
ready? Fasten your space belts—it's the law!
It's time to launch our Space Trip Ship.
10, 9, 8, 7, 6, 5, 4, 3, 2, 1 . . .
Blast off!

238

Today you are in for a treat. We will see Earth, the blue planet.

Look out your window. You can see planet Earth coming closer. Do you see why Earth is called the blue planet? All that blue on it is water. In fact, most of Earth's surface is liquid. The brown and green places are land. You can see white clouds and white patches of ice, too. Sometimes you can even see lightning. Isn't Earth beautiful?

Assemble your Space Scopes, everyone. Look closely at Earth. Do you see all the different kinds of people, animals, and plants? You won't find those on any of the other planets. Only Earth has the air, soil, and water they need. Now turn your Space Scopes to the sun. Be careful—it's awfully bright! The sun's heat is intense. It would be too dangerous for us to visit there. Earth is the third planet from the sun. The planets closer to the sun are too hot for us to live on. Those farther away are too cold. Being the third planet from the sun makes Earth just right for the people, plants, and animals that live on it.

240